Also by JANE DRAYCOTT

Pearl · 2011

Over · 2009

The Night Tree · 2004

Tideway, with Peter Hay · 2002

Prince Rupert's Drop · 1999

Christina the Astonishing, with

Lesley Saunders & Peter Hay · 1998

No Theatre · 1997

JANE DRAYCOTT

The Occupant

CARCANET

First published in Great Britain in 2016 by
CARCANET PRESS LTD
Alliance House, 30 Cross Street
Manchester M2 7AQ
www.carcanet.co.uk

A CIP catalogue record for this book is
available from the British Library.
ISBN 9781784103002

The publisher acknowledges financial assistance
from Arts Council England.

CONTENTS

THE OCCUPANT

for Norman, Holly & Sophie

It's dark in here and forest green: *Britannica,*
sixteen oak trees in a London living room,
the little girl, my mother, in the bookcase glass.
Italy, Ithaca, Izmail, Japan, each page a mainsail
turning, HMS Discovery – *none of the rivers
of southern Italy is of any great importance.*

Like birds on long-haul flight, let not seas
or deserts, cliffs or icy mountain-tops
impede you. Jews, Kabir, Kabul, Kaffir,
from up here all seems clear (*all evil in the world's
ascribed to Maya or illusion*), then home at last
returned from all those navigable miles

to Lichen, Linnet, Logic, London, to find
a century has passed, the forest's cleared,
the animals all bared and scorched, the gold
all brought to light. I look into the glass,
discover there myself in dense shade, deep
and shadowy as on any wooded island.

LOST

'The Emperor of Russia was my father'
Hermione, *The Winter's Tale* (III, ii)

Sleep is a Russian winter in which
you are a girl again – lost, so it seems,
like everything, and turned to stone.
Only your foundling heart still stirs.

Better perhaps to have been born a tree,
to live on summer after summer,
leaves and branches shifting
like a child's hair lifted by the wind.

The wonder is the waking world
is so much like the dream. All's pale,
blank silence, though across the sheet
of snow you almost hear them call:

Astonish us, they seem to say,
astonish us again today.

PROSPECT

Anyone who wanted to could leave, could gather
   shivering on the south side of the river,
labelled and provided for with socks and sweaters
   and a little cash. We walked across the water
in our thousands and left behind forever
   all that was great: the monuments and sewers,
cathedrals, theatres, mothers, lovers, brothers
   as the flames licked at the city's raging heart.

Faced with the prospect of living forever,
   we headed for the country lanes together
imagining the *parties de campagne* among the clover
   and the stories each would tell the others
on the way. We had left behind forever
   all that we had loved. It was a start.

NAMESAKE

'I died a while ago'
R. L. Stevenson, letter to Sidney Colvin, 1879

We ride this train together – the laundered fields, the grass
hoar-frosted like a baker's boy stepped out at dawn.
Inside, we hold our silent winter party, scan
the multiverse and all our doppelgängers there.

Can it be that I am also a firefighter in Texas,
that I have entered blazing warehouses, cut drivers
from their burning cars, searched in the rubble for signs
of the living when all around lay dead or counted lost?

I see your pale face lying in a passing field of frost
and like old Priam wonder, *Ah did my son exist?*
Was he a dream? The rails hand us down the line.
I do not know who it is that is travelling on this train.

Boy in a field, you watch me pass but do not wave.
Could it be if I chose I could be fearless, could be brave?

THE STARE

Outside our block of flats the moon
has planted itself like a searchlight
flooding in through our Indian curtains and neat
Japanese-style blinds, onto the film sets
of all our stacked-up living rooms.

Caught in some small act we are drowned
in its platinum stare (my own room glows,
its forest of furniture, the deep ocean blue
of the carpet) not looking, just letting us know
it's there. After all, life must go on.

Soon it won't just be hanging around
out there, it'll climb right in and carry
this body of mine out into the freezing air,
past the suburbs, the Ministry of Global Affairs,
up to the region of gathering winds.

It'll be like a giant's delicate hand.
It'll be like a winged horse ride.
It'll be like a police searchlight.

That's really something, to see our old blue car
again outside the gate, the lilac still standing,
the date watermarked on the side of the shed.

There's nobody, nobody on that train,
there's nobody on that train.

It's eerily silent. Setting or aftermath, everyone's
staying indoors – that or the cameraman held down
the trigger so long people just disappeared on the street.

I'd like to know – are you, are you in that tunnel?

like Marian, forty, caught on her way to the shops
taken up into vapour and cloud, or the boy with the head
of a horse, stood by the tennis courts waiting.

I'd like to know which animal, animal spoke to me

almost transmuted already, his mane like a fire
of gold, head bowed and hands in his pockets.

Blue, blue's not a colour.

That boy is the one they are looking for,
the gods, coming down our streets at dawn.

WHO KEEPS OBSERVANCE?

Who keeps observance in the fever room?
Around your bed night's cattle-muscle looms.
The deepening countryside's a shower
of coal and ice, machinery's abandoned
in the limitless field. We all could drown.

I have been driving east for days.
In this fenceless county small-town promises
that glow on the horizon are merely zodiacal dust,
false hope derived from outer atmosphere
and particles of skin.
                                          I watch you sweat,
I watch you sleep. Some far and submarine light
keeps you swimming. In the blueberry bloom
lungs loosen, the pulse is in retreat,
speech is unlearned and falls in spools
of oil-shine tape along the mineshaft floor.

It has not always been like this:
imagined light transpires like phantom
sounds discovered in the silence of an armistice –
phytoplankton on the surface of the eye,
loose neon in a side street, fireflies.

Let this cold watch be mine. The heart
creeps down towards the other side of data.
Miles deep a slow wave turns. It will be hours more
before you finally appear, your hair a little longer,
eyes a little paler, wider after what
they've seen. I have been driving east for ever.
I am quite sure that we have lived before.

EACH DAY

*'The poor soul has had a reverse conversion
[...] and will never recover from it'*

Pier Paolo Pasolini, *Medea* (1969)

There's a song I used to know.
I used to jump out of bed in the mornings
singing it like a new recruit ready for the day.
It sounded like an old song from Europe
where the air is so dry and the grass
glittering with the husks of tiny snails.

It was a song about silence, a silence
so profound you could hear cars in it
and trains, and crowds chanting
as they moved like one live beast
slithering down the boulevards.
Avnroiut, it went; and *Henieov*.

All day long I'd have that song
in my head, peeling potatoes, putting
the children to bed, because singing
is good for you in the same way
as birdsong, singing your heart out
from up on the battlements

opening your mouth like a cave
in an arid hillside, the loudest song
you could sing. And now I've taught it
to my children. Otherwise, each day
would be like the Marie Celeste,
as if someone had cast a spell on it.

LOLL-HEAD LETTUCE

Was that gardener someone's father who flying through the doors
of the National Gallery, the wind at his back, shorn
blossoms at his heels, raced down the long halls

of nations, transfigurations and transmigrations of the soul
to cut a clean path to the flowers and the fruit, the insect-life and
    shells
only to stand there, grafting-knife in hand, so rapt and still?

And in his nature-rapture how was that act so private
by which he took the fresh green head, the dew still perfect
in its eye, lifting it from the canvas like a child from a cot

out from among the wine and snuffed-out candles, the ticking
watch and half-devoured pies, so quietly as not to wake it
and nothing in the scene protesting as he walked away?

As he carried it to his garden – sweet lolling head, heart white
with traces of the milky sleep-inducing ooze – to give it life,
another life, I like to think perhaps that father-gardener was mine.

Right now the casement's open to the night
and any creature with a spark of life
could fly right out and still get back to Phoenix.

But this woodland has you in its lure:
the eglantine and roses on the walls,
the swallow and the nightjar all declare

this garden is a place to rest, get back
to nature and to who you really are
beneath those dusty travelling clothes.

Up there above the treeline in a cave
of ice lies a field of untouched snow
and rushing headwaters, the *fons et origo*

that is the farthest any girl should go
alone. No words are spoken here
or can explain what always happens next.

Free-flying in your naked self (and that's
pure pleasure) in the water's rills and tendrils
you're in paradise, like heaven on earth

when, vision or nightmare – it's as close as that –
the spirit of the woods appears to cut you down.
Woodcutter, granny or wolf, it isn't clear –

enough to know that things have gone too far
and all too soon you're with the angels
which is where the money is as well.

And so you end up in the place perpetual
where water is the single syllable that rises
from the ashes, all that lasts after the blast

that comes from nowhere like an August breeze,
comes from beyond the window, from a land
of boiling cloud and altogether bigger trees.

THE OCCUPANT

'...alsof hij hoort waarvan hij droomt
en de plek ziet waar hij te vinden hoopt'

[...as though he hears the thing he's dreamed of
and sees the place he'd hoped to find]

Martinus Nijhoff, 'Awater' (1934)

I

And so because I cannot sleep I leave
the hothouse of my sheets
and walk the streets. How close to me
right now are you? The dead lanes keep
their silence, well-trained in secrecy.
The air's like silk, the trees and street lamps
only like themselves. No dream
could say it clearer. Some compass needle
leads me to the park, where gates of steel
declare, *Each plant and planet feels*
the inmost drive to move and dream.
A young man lies here on a bench, beached
on the night's cool sand – his breathing
falters as I pass. The place is feverish
with noise. A sign, *Menagerie,*
directs me to the regions deep
inside the body of the city,
my ears a stethoscope to its squeals
and ticks, its troubled moans and shrieks.
In their concrete yard the camels' feet
enact some pilgrimage across a sweep
of long-lost dunes, the gilded eagle
listens for the wind-scoured fields

and in the keeper's office floorboards creak,
remembering their former life at sea.
Only the dogs and last night's heat
lie quiet now, their histories deleted.
That's what I'd like my life to be,
not the dream but the young man sleeping.

II

All day becalmed the city sits
at anchor. In Victory Gardens tourists
cram the shady benches, jasmine
shrivels in the back streets, at tills
and kiosks police post notices,
Missing: Have you seen this wind?
The frail expire and pale dogs whimper,
quarantined on this stilled ship.

Just now I thought I saw you slip
a needle's eye through tram doors, singing
as you went. Only that glimpse
and you were gone, invisible,
eclipsed once more by stone and brick.
The heat patrols the precinct,
windows, walls and doorways frisked
in turn. The sun's eye never blinks.

I pray for a miraculous pitch
of snow. Across the road a cinema
beckons, EXIT — WAY IN
the doors revolve, *this way for winter*
they seem to say. It's like a fridge

in here, the inside of a kiss
made cool by ice and gin. I swim
into its darker water, swallowed in.

The film's set in some future city –
narrowed skies, the air electric,
a chase scene through a crowd spilled out
across a pavement, late-night drinking.
And then I see you there amid
the extras, as if you'd walked in
from the street and been uplifted
to the screen, its living window.

You seem so happy there. What is
that world? So much I'd never noticed
I see now – how tall and willowy
you've grown, the way your spirit flickers
between eyes and lips. Film
does that, the focus on the face, the skin.
Out on the dimming street a stirring's
in the air, a breath from somewhere distant
as though a storm had flapped a wing.

III

Boarding the tram was like taking my place
on the back of the mythical serpent, that tale

of citizens carried along the lanes
in open daylight, watched from gables

and roof-lights by neighbours who gazed
amazed as the dragon snaked them away.

'Better to travel than arrive,' you always say
so I sing to keep my spirits raised.

We have come to a region of skyscrapers,
giant redwoods of glass that sway

under the clouds. We have come to a place
I never dreamed so close, so strange.

It seems like forever. We are going to tame
the storm and sea. I cannot wait.

IV

Raised on the storm-farm he roams
the horizon, lamplighter far from home
powering through cloud's blown
sail, close to overload. Some woeful
wrong-doing done, some woe
to raise electrodes in the throat.
Then, cinema inferno,
white water solders
down the sky's sheer stone
and rain comes molten.
Furious now he throws
it all in the firepit. So
the house blows wholly open.

Our street's a shallow sound, water no wider
than a child might wade to cross its sudden tide.
The city falling shivers on its shine
and in our rows of lighthouses we climb
the stairs to keep the lantern rooms alight.
Where in all this rain are you? The grapevine
says you're sleeping out in fields at night,
miles from these dogs and sirens. Beside
the presidential palace some imp or sprite
left over from the storm is tugging wildly
at the flag like a looter in a riot. This time
last year it fluttered at half-mast – *Like a giant
bending low*, you said and wiped
away a tear for whoever must have died.
Perhaps, you said, *the family are at the graveside
now or making tea at home*, and I replied
At times like this some people like to be outside,
not shut up in their cockpit of a fire-tower
in case tonight should be the night
(and this is in a dream) you cycle by
and wave to me across the stream's divide.
I'll wait until the dogs bark five more times
and five more cars – our ministers, scientists,
generals – roll down the palace drive,
then ride out to the dunes and find you
lying in the fine long grasses, fine for miles.
The restless grasses, restless, moving, fine.

So Many Things

Scaling the heights I saw how each glazy eye
was a room, duplicate save for the nameplates
on the doors, places where only the trafficking light
ever entered, teetering over the streets arraigned
below. I perceived how sunlight sparked and fired
there, and seeds like hail thrashed the laminate
and raindrops ran like liquor.

         I observed how the fly
saw everything, its drone kingdom luminous, rarefied
above the multitude who in their exceeding sadness gazed
and wondered about the ingenious magnitude of space.

I saw more visions: frozen ferns and flames, a paradise
of scales and grain, so many things explained
though never any clue about the rooms, the eyes
where furniture might have been or love or any real trade.

WHERE IS YOUR BANKSMAN?

You wait in the cab of the excavator
but he's nowhere to be seen, head down
somewhere in his copy of *Aerial News*. *The sky's the future*,
he says, and that's where he is now, missing again,

gone hang-gliding, abseiling from skyscrapers,
soaring from the cliff at the top of the world,
captain marvellous. *Up there you feel more alive*, he says,
more human – take it on trust – *closer to God*.

You miss him though you never really saw his face
under the helmet, watched only for his magician's hands.
So it's always sunny in the stratosphere, what use
is high-wire walking when help is needed on the ground?

The earth lies opened-up in front of you, clay and stone.
Tomorrow he'll return like Marco Polo to give
the world detailed account of all the lands he's seen
invisible to you. How much of it can you believe?

SENSATION

'*say that my answer was, RECALLED TO LIFE*'
Charles Dickens, *A Tale of Two Cities*

Two nights, two roads, two hills,
two reeking fogs, two passageways
dimly lit, two persons.

Among those terrors concealed
in the darkness something golden,
something *blazing strange*.

Awake by a small fire a person
in interview with himself: across
in the darkness some truths revealed.

Two fires lit on a foreshore,
the shore stretching only as far
as the fires allow. Two men.

Rowing in from the darkness a man
or a man and a boy or a young man alone.
A small fire. In sight, two persons.

THE WATCHIE

Joan Eardley RSA, *Coastline at Catterline*

The vast was a wavelift of rocksand,
sunlight and water in uproar, bluff
where the wind slipped ahead of its leash.

And the wash contained cities: tunnels
and galleries, pillars and bridges, outlands
with quarry tracks running for miles.

From the Watchie you watched – exuberant tides,
the cliff with its heat store like honey – and wanted
to cling to its skirts, its foot-holes and handholds,
the warmth in the stone of its pockets.

In the evening, like the mind breaking up,
there came static: landslip and fleetwreck,
shores ragged and dredged,
the sea loose in the little museum.

Those nights, you stood on the coast path,
the stuff itself in your eyes – mica and moss,
and in your mouth windspeed and whiplash

its charge and its mass – unable to see in the dark
how large or small you might be or how vast the vast.

ARRIVA BUS

'his most troubling thought, that perhaps he had taken the wrong road'
Henri Alain-Fournier, *Le Grand Meaulnes* (1913)

It is my intention once past the carpet
warehouses and one-stop hotels to look out
for signs: cart tracks, mist on the fields,
a stream running on under ditch-ice,
the mare plodding patiently onward –

maybe a churchyard where somebody learned
to read from the gravestones, after which
they had at their fingertips all the great classics
of literature, and perhaps a sea of green wheat
in which I can swim and keep swimming

after which I'll take the road back one day,
some book unopened on my lap, because everyone
has to have somewhere to come home from.
I hope it will be like coming back down through
the clouds, to earth from a far town called Cloud.

WE MUST NOT THINK OF HIM

'the tower became his lair...'
Château de Montaigne

We must not think of him sitting
            but walking, great thinker
pacing, eyes lifted to the ribs
            of rafters, bird's wing pinned
and fanned, inscribed with maxims
            left to cure five hundred winters.
We watch him swim
            his lengths: philosophy, religion,
history, and we are pinioned.

Above our heads our child is sitting
            in the sky, British Airways shimmying
her away, long steady strokes while bits
            of us fly with her, scrips
of kindred rising on the wind.
            Our only aim is to outlive this visit,
back down past the spiral windows
            to catch her trail, new thoughts lifting
each with its beautiful ticket.

THE DRIVE

All the way home in the car
he'd been playing the memory game:
money, crisps, smartphone, knife,
the things he'd pack in a suitcase.
The boy had asked to see the sea
so we'd driven until we saw it,
three hours' crawl out the city, that's
what I'd call love, till we reached the land
of corn and beehives and big hanging clouds
to get to the beach at somewhere-on-sea.

He'd stood on the shingle but wouldn't
go near. I told him, stop being afraid.
Over there, and I pointed across
at the slow quiet brute of the sea,
is another shore just like this one,
with a boy standing there but braver
than you. And wading in I'd shown him how.
Now up in his bedroom he's staring,
There, he says. *Now I can see it.*
Staring at all we'd ever given him.

Noon and no-one's on the street
except the girl. No shade to stain
the stonework, the light so bright
the traffic lights are sightless.

They're all away, tending
to their estates. Item: hedging,
laurel, box; item: boathouse, landing
stages. Crossing the meridian,
a single windhover minds the ridge.

A window opens in the Ministerium –
mappa mundi, one set of cameras
for the whole piazza, no such thing as away.

The morning's wiped, the cash machine's
impossible to read, on-screen statements
your reflection only.
                              In this gorgeous glare
bones grow and muscles lengthen –
a girl could climb to her full height.

The sun-ship yaws. Its locker doors,
flown open, spill the jewel store. She stares.

As high as it gets on the day's hill the kestrel
checks its kill. You can make this happen.
The view was never better than from here,
and later when you close your eyes, still there.
This is what you look like from the air.

Teas are served in the library.
I watch the tablecloth, its snowy
flowerprint, consume you at your sleeve.
Outside, the gardens swarm: men
and women emerging from the soil
catch fire and form while others slither
into the beds like snakes of molten glass,
shutting the little doors behind them in the lawn.

You say the bookcase is a secret door.
If ever lost in thought or contemplation
you slip too far into the cloth or wallpaper
like Narcissus into his pool, please
beware. I do not want to lose you,
run with arms outstretched toward a cloud
of vapour, trying to embrace you
long after you've turned into a tree.

Let's put an end to disappearing,
reappearing as a constellation, cold
and distant, a frightened stag at bay.
Come out from behind that half-closed
door so I can see you clearly
amid the fire, the blizzard in this room.

WESTERNAYS

for Bernard

is when your car ends facing backwards
    on the wrong side of the road

when the wind beats your umbrella
    till its insides all hang out

when the water takes your little boat
    and spins it like a plate.

It's like a song reversed, a church
    constructed widershins

to face the falling sun, the day
    next week or sometime soon

you'll take a truth and twist it,
    turn a child to face the wall.

It's the dream which has you driving
    down exactly the wrong street

as you race to reach your boat
    before it sails.

It's the wind along the western quay,
    the voices in its throat

the seaman on the closing doors,
    the words you hear him shout

I'll wait. I'll wait all night
        if need be. I can wait.

LAKE

Right now I'm at my lake and you're
at yours. Everyone knows
about lakes with villages in them,
church and all. If I dived
like Beowulf into the mere, down
through the cellars and ice-houses,
beneath stalactites called *the cathedral*,
the crypt, *the green chapel*, could I
surface in your lake and see you there
reading, sipping your beer in the sun
on the underside of the world?
Some people have whole lake-worlds
in their heads, like the boy-prince who lay
with his small face bent to the lake
near the palace trying to glimpse
the children at the bottom. I could
have told him, just keep swimming
with your eyes, past the mouth
of the dreadful cave, till you see them.
Don't take them off the water.

ATLAS

for H & S

All day he waited in the corner of the top field
where the signal was strongest. Beetles
and ladybirds led their lives round his feet.
Celandines, poppies, Michaelmas, snow.
Gone for a season, they'd said. He looked
through binoculars west toward the drystone
borders of central America, the reefs,
volcanoes and fruit trees, straining to see it,
the island where everyone went barefoot.

He wanted to ask, are there snakes
in the orchard, do strangers come by on the path,
are you frightened at night? At the end of the day
he saw them, the sky's door half open, lit up
over Marriot's Wood like fire on a beach.
He'd taught them how you could turn a map
underworld-up and it still be the Earth.
Looking back at the house he saw how even
the roof he'd raised for them all was a boat.

THE RETURN

Accident has brought them together,
the grand piano and the single chair
listening in the abandoned sanatorium
for night's quiet breathing, its *va et vient*
across the shoreline of the window.

They are waiting for winter to sail in
along the straits of lime trees, for its ghost
to flow through them into the house,
the rooms where clouds will gather,
rose-spotted paintwork peeling softly,
half-moon fanlights rising, sinking.

They can never forget summer, wheeled
onto the terrace to catch the sun,
music like fluid in the air, the walks
between the colonnades of leaves,
the talk, the friendships and the brief affairs.

Like animals on a darkened field
they watch for the returning patient,
her fevered hair, her voice of thinnest ice,
carried in as always by her father
the sea. Everything that happens starts
and finishes in that avenue of trees.

SONG FOR WULF

after *The Exeter Book*

To my people he'd be like a gift   easy prey
if he dared to come armed,   the man they would love to destroy.
     So we live in our separate worlds

Wulf on one island   I on another,
this fastness encircled   by marsh and fen,
this island of blood-thirsty   battle-hard men
who'd love to destroy him   if ever he dared to come armed.
     So we live in our separate worlds.

In my thoughts I follow   his far-trailing footsteps
while rain continues to fall   and I sit here keening
wound fast in the circling   warrior arms of another,
each thought   weighing equal measures
     of pleasure and pain.

Wulf, my own Wulf   I am weak
from thinking of you   in your overlong absence,
the grief in my heart   far greater
     than any hunger for food.

Remember Eadwacer, warrior: it's easy
to sever those ties   never truly united.
Remember that Wulf   has carried our unhappy cub
away   into the woods – the song
     he and I made together.

MILESTONE

At this milestone rest   after all that
   racing about   torch-leaves
down on the ground for you   small red boats
   gathered there   the empty public road.

By this milestone wait   your bare feet
   on the stone's stone   your face tipped up
to catch a bit of sun   your resting heart
   dissolving   even in simple rainwater.

Fare thee well   our hearts like brooches
   hung from the trees.   How far can you be?

AFTER HENRI MICHAUX

1. I am Gong

In the song of my anger lies an egg
and in that egg lie my mother and my father and my children,
and happiness and sadness mixed, and life,
fierce storms that gave me shelter,
the lovely sun that blocked my path.

Inside me there is hatred – ancient, strong.
As for beauty, time will tell. Truth is,
I've grown harder layer by delicate layer.
If you could only know how soft I am inside,
I am cotton wool and gong and deepest snow song.

This I am certain of and do declare.

II. Out on the Lane to Death

Out on the lane to Death
my mother came across a great floe.
She wanted (it was already
getting late) to speak.
A vast cotton-wool field of ice.
She looked at us, my brother and me,
and then she cried.

We told her – truly absurd lie –
we understood her perfectly.
And then she smiled
her charming young girl's smile, the one
that was the real her.
Her pretty, almost mischievous smile.
After which she was taken into the great Opaque.

THIS STORM

This storm tonight has really stirred
people up. The street's deserted,

cleared for the marathon of the wind,
the dry twigs setting off hotfoot,

the river of dead leaves lively as anything
racing for the woods and home.

Remember how you used to search
the forests, even in your dreams?

How you said that what by day seemed
muddied, hidden like mushrooms

in the tangy earth, by night
seemed clearer, like a running stream?

Hearing of your death today has got me
thinking about how much I liked you.

THE HILL ABOVE HARLECH:
WILLIAM NICHOLSON 1917

'No person shall [...] make any photograph, sketch, plan,
model or other representation within any area...'
Defence of the Realm Act, January 1916

The landscape was on the radio. It was early days transmitting
like that but some things came through – the fields, the shine
of the slate roofs after the rain. The artist added his voice:

a map was the last thing he'd wanted to make from the smoke
near the cottages crouched by the wood, the crawl of the shadows
out from under the walls, the light the colour of tin.

But it was all words. He'd wanted to show how the sky
was everything, the pandemonium and the lulls
in the pandemonium. The slow march home, the long road.

Silent Movie

The scene requires you to cry and you want to.
What you need is buried somewhere
deep in the woods by the lakeside, stored

in the sap or lodged in the branches there
between shoulder and ribcage when you move
like this or carry your hand to your mouth.

It helps to imagine some music inside you,
your own music eaten alone in the past
or the cold grey song of a stranger.

What works best is a change in weather –
no more talk of picnics on the little sandy beach,
just armies of cloud rolling in again noiselessly.

A third is always lost to melting
but still he climbs each morning
in the jiggling dark, frail now, more bird
than man. As he stows his cargo light
steals up around him like a watching crowd
Then down like Moses among the bluffs
and contours, villages where no-one lives
but clocks still chime and finches chatter on.
Can it be true? they say and say.
Miles below, the coast lies drowsing,
tired from too much love and heartbreak.
The hospitals and fishermen, the restaurants
and bars, all waiting for him there.
He knows they'll run to it like something lost,
close their eyes and sigh at what
he's brought, a taste of sky and stone.
He will not come again tomorrow.
The mountains do not care how beautiful they are.

THE WINTER HOUSE

a carol

In winter's house there's a room
that's pale and still as mist in a field.
Outside on the street every gate's shut firm,
every face as cold as steel.

In winter's house there's a bed
that's spread with frost and feathers, and gleams
in the half-light like rain in a disused yard
or a pearl in a choked-up stream.

In winter's house there's a child
who's asleep in a dream of light, growing out
of the dark, a flame you can hold in your hand
like a flower, or a torch on the street.

In winter's house there's a tale
that's told of a great chandelier in the garden,
of fire that catches and travels for miles,
of windows and gates left open.

In winter's house there's a flame
being dreamt by a child in the night,
in the small quiet house at the turn in the lane
where darkness gives way to light.

Rosa 'Madame A. Meilland' (Peace)

for Peter Scupham

You could in the last of daylight cultivate a rose
and name it for your mother. A ship in the bay
might sail with it. On the dockside gantry and willow
could bow their heads. But no known prayer or herb
can prevent the coming night's invasion nor fire
from flowering there now fear is a spreading weed.

You could watch the child by the railway who knows
all there is to know about weeds and fire, the way
the bayonets and flaming spires can swallow
a field in one. This is the new wild tribe –
from the bank they feel the metal's heat, the power
at which a night-time can approach and pass, its speed.

LENT

The bailiff winds are at the door.
Alcohol and cigarettes must go. Abstain,
repent. No meat, no chocolate, no more
obsessive checking of your phone
like the pulse of a dying friend. Refrain.
No more taking photographs of pictures.
Let the world go like Michelangelo's sculpture
made of snow that no-one framed.

The house lies purged and empty. Still the winds blow.
Now give up the wilderness, the wandering.
Retreat instead to that windless winter morning
when a young man stood in the gardens of the palazzo,
lips glistening, hair shining at the nape
before the bomb-blast of sun, not anyone's to keep.

MEETING MARGARET

i.m. P. B.D.

Meeting Margaret off the train
is like greeting the wind.
Stepping down she smiles
as if she's been smiling all the while
since you parted, in her sleep,
at work, cleaning her teeth.

In her outstretched hands
she holds a ship curled like a cat
asleep in her arms, masts
down but ready to sail at the first
call. *I'm going on a cruise*,
she says. *Come with me, please.*

You want to ask her something
but you just take the ship from her,
wriggling like the four winds
in your hands. *Haven't we met
somewhere?* And then she's off
in full sail swirling along the quay.

Traditional wedding dish of lamb
and apricots, fresh spices, almonds;
a prayer-like gesture with the hands;
in Scandinavia, to place a candle
in a window at the year's end.

Faced with a word deep-fathomed
from an ancient sea-chest we all as family
consider. In the room the world expands
around us, ice-falls, uplands,
squares and villages, verandas.

At last the dripping chest is opened:
Icelandic woollen fishing hat (slang:
cap worn by executioner or hangman)
green water frozen from the dawn
of time, smelling of the dark and plankton

micro-organisms from which we all descend,
the fishermen moving among us, outlandish.

Returned one day from who knows where
you'll climb the stairs, each step a flight
into the roof-space, to a room which like
a lover waits: some books, a sofa, perfect light,
the soft green carpet like a grassy hill
though in truth the books are flat and dull

and written in a language you can't read,
so all that's left's to lie out on that knoll and,
gazing through the branches and their leaves,
listen to the noise of tackle and hardware
coming across the lawns, and to the sound
of chickens, of the many geese that she'll

be keeping, her crying, all that night and day
whenever it may be.

SLEEPERS

In one small house the blizzard enters
a woman's bedroom, fierce eyes blue
beneath the frozen brow and hair, fingers
cool and delicate along the streams
and branching rivers of her skin.

When he is done he takes his leave
without a word, picks up his maps and compass,
calls his obedient dogs. She'd like to follow,
but a dream is not an ice-ship,
cannot take her anywhere.

At their window every sleeper stands,
surveys the surface since the frost
gave way. Inside their heads the world
is white again, has nothing still to say.
The whole town dreams the same dream.

It is after the war is over. You are sleeping under
the ankles of hedges, the map clear above you,
the hunter, the beasts of the heavens all on the move.

No such thing anymore as frontiers or borders,
debatable lands. Old charts are unrolled,
the world on the back of a calf – arterial blood
for the Red Sea, veins for the rivers and coasts.

Where you walk pigeons' wings are a waterwheel
turning. The creak of a pram is a door slowly closed.
Indoors you stand by the window waiting for dawn.
What you see is yourself, when you move she is gone.

Skies burn. The trees have their thoughts. The animals
wander through gaps in the hedges and left-open gates.
These are the thoughts you cannot complete.

AT REMENHAM

for Matt & Louise

Lift an oar from out the water, wipe the shadow
from the moon, raise a head from off a pillow
or a bucket from the snow – take all these things away
and what's left is a perfect *oh* or love, a loop,
a ring, an eye to turn the world the right way up,
a guiding lens for tracking stars while far at sea.

It's the path around a sundial, a circle made of stone
where things happen once and yet were always so.
It's both centre and circumference, both spyglass
and moon. Whichever way you turn it, it's the focus
where the fire at the heart of all things burns.

AERODROME

Not the words that were lost on the wind,
the multitude prone on the tarmac, his voice
like a voice from a distant echoing cave.

Not the hundred thousand cheap lighters raised
as an answering beacon, the uncanny shimmer
surrounding his head, the death of the moon.

Remind us instead of the tongues of fire
we saw by the roadside that night, the visions
that curled like snakes from our tangled hair,

the veteran flight sergeant, burning coals
in his eyes, who stopping to give us a ride
said, *Write of the things thou hast seen*

and drove away down the A31 on the flaming wings
of an eagle, our dark hills and low world revealed.

IT WON'T BE LONG

With the Beatles
(Parlophone, 22 November 1963)

Here comes the sun, though it's November
and half the globe's in darkness still.
The world's in black and white though colour's
just around the corner. Our mother's ill,
her half-moon face towards the wall,
but Father you are cooking curry, Vesta
where the hearth is though no-one's
even thought of going to India yet.
What is this shadow? Come together now.
With easy rice, with every good intention,
with navy trim, with matching pillbox hat.
We are with you Father in the kitchen,
we are all together. The day's half gone,
the moon is up and Mother's coming down
to help you cook. Soon there will be rice
all over the place. Here comes the heat.
It's midday now in Dallas and it won't be long.
Stuff you couldn't put a name to all over the place.

Almighty god who made the land
and sea but did not make these canals,
look down from your attic at this latticework
of water, how in the dank and damp
a barge's bow-lamp scans the embankment.

See how the star-spoked web expands,
a sash round the city's waist, there where the hand
rests close to the heart like Rembrandt's Isaac
and his young Rebecca, his sleeve a match-flame,
living sun and honeycomb alive on the canvas.

The fingers of the water fan out
in their channels, search the darkening map.
Where is she now, the girl? Hold the candle
closer to this patch of night, its amber
heart observed from any watching planet.

AUCTION

I had bid for the lot, the panes of high-grade glass,
the frame of steel, the sprinkler pipes, orchids and ferns,
the ventilation grilles shaped like sun and moon.

I'd been wandering the city looking for love and just called
in off the street. It seemed like a fine way to live, walls
you could see through, waving to strangers as one human being
to another, a roof to see straight to the clouds and stars.

Life without curtains, no shame and nothing to hide.
Like love in the blitz, fireplaces hung in the sky,
chandeliers dangling from rafters freed
from the dark rooms above and below. It seemed

like everything I'd been looking for, a house
of glass, to wake at four a.m. and look night
in the eye. I thought I had wanted nothing less.

THE LITTLE HOUSE

Inside you lies a second human heart
that's dreaming of a house that could be built:
a tiny staircase, two small fireplaces,
a painted floor and *trompe l'oeil* balcony,
a miniature roof-light open to the sky.
Outside the door's an orchard lit with fruit
which scattered on the ground spell *welcome, eat.*

Sparked by love your extra bird heart flies
inside a month or two, no more.
Still vestiges of the house remain – some tiles,
the outline of a formal garden, traces
of a small face at a window, eyes,
an arm and fingers clearly visible,
details it will be a life's work to restore.

Acknowledgements are due to the following publications, where some of these poems first appeared: *The Arts of Peace* (ed. Adrian Blamires & Peter Robinson, Two Rivers Press, 2014); *Ash Magazine*; *The Captain's Tower* and *Newspaper Taxis* (ed. Phil Bowen, David Furniss & David Woolley, Seren, 2011, 2013); *The Guardian; Joining Music with Reason* (ed. Christopher Ricks, Waywiser Press, 2010); *Literary Review*; *Magma*; *Manhattan Review*; *Modern Poetry in Translation*; *molossus*; *A Mutual Friend: Poems for Charles Dickens* (ed. Peter Robinson, Two Rivers Press, 2013); *Of Love and Hope* (ed. Deborah Gaye, Avalanche, 2010); *Oxford Poetry Centenary Issue*; *Poetry London*; *The Poetry Review*; *The Rialto*; *The Stephen Spender Prize Anthology, 2010*; *The Times Literary Supplement*; *Tokens for the Foundlings* (ed. Tony Curtis, Seren, 2012); *Writers on Writing* (ed. Amal Chatterjee, C&H, 2013).

'Lost' was commissioned as part of Liverpool University's *The Winter's Tale Festival* 2011; 'The Shower Scene' and 'Each Day' were part of the British Film Institute's *Psycho Poetica* (2010) and *Poets on Pasolini: A New Decameron* (2013) devised by Simon Barraclough; 'The Winter House' was included in Poet Laureate Carol Ann Duffy's 'Carols for Christmas', *The Guardian*, 2010; 'The Watchie' and 'Remembered Land: Victoria Crowe, 1999' were contributions to Reading Museum's *A Sense of Place* exhibition, 2015–16, curated by Lesley Saunders & Elaine Blake; 'Noon and No-one' and 'Who Keeps Observance?' were commissioned for Jaybird Live Literature / The Poetry Society's *Beginning to See the Light*, 2015–16.

I am extremely grateful to the Society of Authors for an Authors' Foundation Award, and to the Dutch Foundation for Literature (NL Letterenfonds) for the grant of time as Writer in Residence, Amsterdam, in 2013, especially to Thomas Möhlmann for all his encouragement and help. My warm thanks also to Caroline and David, for their much-valued hospitality in allowing me to stay so often in such a perfect place to work.